Life as I know it

Faye Hart

BookLeaf
Publishing

India | USA | UK

Presentation by *BookLeaf Publishing*

Web: www.bookleafpub.com

E-mail: info@bookleafpub.com

ISBN: 9789358315523

First edition 2023

DEDICATION

To my darling husband, without your support I would be lost.

To my mum, who's creativity has helped me flourish.

To my sister and her unwavering love.

To my children, who see the best intentions for all that I do... Keep aiming high.

Love you all xxx

New Life

The shrill cry of lungs taking their first breath
Of the cold reality of life outside the pulsing
bubble
The silence of the world
No mothering heartbeat or gushing of blood
Silence

Warm hands cradling you
Voices you have only known from afar
Louder now but somehow still comforting

Everything is so big when you're so little
The world is louder now
All startling
Curling up, be smaller
Suddenly so much space

But mummy and daddy have you
Nestled in their arms
Surrounded by their love

This moment is brought back to family members
who may have forgotten the newborn love
The innocence and purity in the cry and sigh

Your name a whispered secret,
A soft dedication to lost love
Pride swelling the chest.
Tears fall
Life will never be the same again
It'll be so much better...

Hands that talk

In the journey of life,
We have whispered many things,
Thought and dreams,
Nightmares and fears.

But life has dealt you a funny hand,
'hearing loss related to old age'
Only 20% hearing in your left ear.

The blow has been swift and un-nerving,
Conversations have changed,
We can't talk in the car without me bellowing,
You move me to the right side of your body.

We negotiate it all together so the decisions has
been made...

We'll learn a new language,
We'll quieten our voice,
Moving our hands in swift motions,
Our lips mimicking what we need to say

British Sign Language
Is our new adventure together,
So we don't lose our connections.

The Art of Poetry

Words spill onto the page,
Murmurings of thoughts given the light of day,
Showing the inner workings of my mind.

Feelings...
Thoughts...
Wishes...
Dreams...
Nightmares...

Do I want it to rhyme?
Do I want the reader to sympathise?
Does it need to be a sonnet or haiku?
Do I need all of these rhetorical questions?
What would Shakespeare do?

There isn't a right or wrong way to do it,
Spill your guts for all to see,
Keep the bits you want for yourself but are you
authentic to the process?

It is an art...
That some people don't get,
And some people pretend they do,
When they have no bloody idea.

It can be as strong as a wave and the darkness of shade.
But it's yours to do with as you see fit

Who cares if they don't get it?

Tornado in the Kitchen

The flurry of activity,
steam from the hob,
oven full blast,
swirling smells drifting down corridors
    and stairs.

Tummies rumbling,
anticipating the feast.

Plates clatter as the table is set.
Drinks orders met.

Chairs scrape on the wooden floor.
The baby shouting for more.

Knives and forks picked up quickly,
Ketchup and salt distrubuted liberally.

Silence takes over the room,
munching and crunching as loud as
    horses chewing hay!

Bath time

The splashing of water
The giggle and gaggle of children,
having a wail of a time,
the laughter is infectious.

Grown ups grumble, no water on the floor
as the youngest fills up the boat and pours it
over the side

Towels on the radiator,
warming to be put onto shivering bodies
toothpaste at the ready on colourful toothbrushes

The water gurgles as it escapes down the
plughole,
taking the day's play away,
taking away the grass stains and crumbs of food.

The smell of shampoo drifts off heads and pjs
are snuggly...
Sleep tight little ones
New adventures await in the morning
X x X

Galaxies and beyond

The shifting of light dancing on the ceiling,
lulling, tugging, cajoling you to the land of
dreams...
Seering scarlet shimmers in symphony until the
emerging emerald exudes energy that exchanges
into
wisps of water washing away the green.

The colours constantly shift,
morph,
Like dancing whispers refracting light and
emotion.
The reminder that the colours are all one and
separate,
that we are one and separate too

Our lives mingle for a time,
and tint our outlook on life forever,
the turns we took together and the drifting apart.

Galaxies and life's complexities
shift and evolve,
dimensions change
manipulates time
as if it never happened or wasn't there,
but the feeling remains.

Puzzle Pieces

What if we were all just a puzzle piece?
Destined to find those who fit us
and sifting through those who don't.

The curves and the straight bits,
never knowing until we're too far in, if they suit
us and how we work.

Should we have a sign to show the shape we
fill?
How could we begin to know?

What if you're so desperate to fit that you start
cutting pieces off?
Turning a curve into a straight bit and cutting
through the straight to create a curve?

And despite having changed so much there are
gaps,
slithers of light filtering through
and you obviously don't fit together.

Life is a journey to find:
your shape
your fit

your people
your love
don't adapt yourself to fit those who don't suit,
they need to compliment you...
See your true worth.

When our body is tired

When our body is tired,
We can't fight off the gunk,
We fill up and store the germs,
Until the very rim...

Then our body gives up,
When our body is tired,
It can't subdue the urge to crawl into bed,
The coughing that begins to hurt our head,
The fire that courses through our veins and
results in damp clothes and soggy hair
Or musty air surrounding us like a shieid.

Vapour rub is our new perfume,
Hands, pockets and bags stuffed with tissues,
both used and clean,
Swiping at our noses causing it to reddened and
flake.

No amount of blowing taking away the tickles in
the ears or the frog stuck at the back of our
throats.

When our body gives up and succumbs to the
illness, the sickness, the plague.

We try to take it easy,
But never before we're sick...

Only...
When our body is tired.
Then you can finally
rest.

We are meant to be guardians

The concrete jungle
Buildings taller than trees,
Standing where there used be carbon dioxide
converters of the highest kind

Stripped away to make space for us
a plague across the planet
using and abusing all in our path.

Erasing habitats,
green lands, wooded areas and forcing animals
to adapt...
But worse than that,
Destroying the rotating ball we call home.

We have a duty to care for where we live,
beyond just ourselves,
beyond our needs,
we are the guardians of the only planet we know
of to have life.

Food with laughter

To share a meal
Lovingly cooked with children underfoot and
chaos all around

But the children fade as the night draws on
Bedtime for all
Some happy to go to bed
The littlest fights sleep always
except
when you want him to stay
awake in the car to go to
bed at home
cue eye roll

Wonderful praises for the food you mushed
together
so much so that as the dishes are cleared
a guest grabs the serving bowl and swipes with
the spare roti
We don't live on ceremony here

Laughter and chatter drifts around
the night turns late and you need to leave
Thank you for coming all this way,
Let's do this again soon

Your world

The world you are born into is very small
It consists of 2 people, maybe three
you and mum, and dad

then your world gets bigger,
you're introduced to more people
and your world gets bigger

but you still revolve around mum,
she is your sun
your safety
your security

you get bigger
growing over time and
your world gets bigger again
you have a personality
make friends
go to school
but your world still revolves around mum.

Time passes slowly and quickly
the days fly by and drag

At some point you'll be grown and then the
world wont revolve around mum any more
you will find a new centre
a new sun

Just remember that I will always be here
a pair of safe arms
a hand to hold
a heart to hear as you snuggle in.

Noises

Whimpering of the dog wanting to be cuddled
Worbling of a child singing in the shower
Swishing of the dishwasher getting rid of the last
meal
Humming of the fridge storing the next meal
Creak of the chair as you shift on the seat
Ding of the doorbell notification of guests

The world is loud and in our face,
we need to find a way to turn it down

Us House

Us house
we packed up our house,
your things went into boxes
then we moved to Grandma and Grandad's

See we bought a new house,
but it wasn't fit to live in,
so we moved to Grandma and Grandad's

You still shared a room with Merryn
so that much hadn't changed but you didn't know
the different between us living with Grandma
and Grandad
and us living in the new house

so you called the new house
us house
and us house became a thing

it was something you could hold on to
to talk about and
so very YOU

In us house you would have your own room,
in us house you could play on the floor,

in us house you would have a big boy bed
in us house you could run circles around the
ground floor,
being chased by the girls

We got to move into us house,
an inconceivable length of time for you,
6 months later,
with lots of hard work from our family who love
us,
grandad gave us hot water and heating,
grandpa made the kitchen,
daddy poured his love into every room
to make us a home
an us house

Why I write

Why I write is to ease the pain,
the pain of life,
and all that is thrown at me.

-

It is a completely selfish act,
for me, myself and I,
to see my words in print

and to share,
much like others have done with me.

Train

Movement, Destinations.

Starting, Changing, Stopping.

Daily commute to work.

Travel.

Following Instructions

I pick up the box,
pull of the wrapper.

The instructions enclosed,
tossed aside.

~

People tell you how to live,
behave, dress.

~

What about your instructions?
lost in the making,
screwed in the wash.

~

I don't do well being told what to do.
I'm sure that it would be stated in my
instructions,

If only they could be found....

Freedom

I need to stretch my body,
pop the joints,
pull the muscles,
shed the skin.
    Pound the pavement,

    Walk,

    Run,

    Flee.

Change my direction,
Free myself
from the ties of life.

    Explode,

    Explore,

    Discover.

Find a lost lake,
Discover the Golden City,
Shake off my shackles.

To return to my home,

To safety,

To Reality.

Box

I am a box,
To be filled,
To be emptied.
Plain packaging,
Big, small, medium,
Covered in writing,
Blank.

To be picked up,
Put aside,
Forgotten about.
Torn,
Flattened down,
Thrown away,
Recycled.

I recognise my own wealth,
I see my potential,
The ability to brush off,
Start again.

I am a box,
Something to be updated,
Knowledge,
Truth,
Pleasure.

I am a box,
Unique in every single way.
One of a kind,

Lose me and I am lost forever.

My Faye

You were very little
when your dad and I met,
you didn't really speak
but could say 'ay' eventually.

It was never my intention
to replace your mum

As time went on
you stopped correcting people,
when they called me mum
and just went with it.

At church one day,
aged about three
a girl you were playing with
pointed out her mum who I was talking to
you pointed and said
    there's my Faye...

Doesn't everyone have a Faye?

would recommend

Repetition

As a parent you go through phases
of repeated phrases.

Thank you
Please
Yes and no.

Up the stairs
downstairs go.

I try my best to help you speak,
but for a chunk of time your anger shows,
unable to understand what you mean,
your cheeks reach a red peek.

Your words are coming
your favourite though is mama.

It is a blessing and a curse
for mama to be heard over and over
over and over again.

No Thomas, time for sleep
lie down,
back to bed,
it's ok, I'm still here.

Helping you to learn to speak...
As a parent you go through phases
of repeated phrases.

What's in a name?

Faye
That's how it started
you had a mum and now I'm with your daddy

Mummy
I had the privilege of growing you
you've heard my heart from the inside
room mates for 9 months and 4 days

Aunty Faye
We wanted you here with family and not with
strangers
you had a rough start
but have been so trusting that we have your best
intentions in mind.
I've been promoted to mummy now

Mama
we don't know what you'll be like yet,
arriving at a precious 3 days old...
a bundle of energy
creating chaos wherever you go
but I'll be Mama forever.

www.ingramcontent.com/pod-product-compliance
Lightning Source LLC
LaVergne TN
LVHW021331200726
843509LV00014B/2491